THE
BEAUTY
BENEATH

Unmasking the Realities of
LIPO, 360 TUMMY TUCKS
AND BBL FAIRYTALES

LATOYA JOHNSON

S.H.E. PUBLISHING, LLC

The Beauty Beneath : Unmasking the Realities of Lipo 360,
Tummy Tucks and BBL Fairytales.
Copyright © 2024 by Latoya Johnson

For information contact:

info@shepublishingllc.com or visit
www.shepublishingllc.com

Cover and Title Page Design by Michelle Phillips of CHELLD3
3D VISUALIZATION AND DESIGN

ISBN: 978-1-964061-15-3 (*paperback*)

First Edition: September 2024
10 9 8 7 6 5 4 3 2 1

Disclaimer

"WHILE IT IS WISE TO LEARN FROM EXPERIENCE, IT IS WISER TO LEARN FROM THE EXPERIENCES OF OTHERS." [Rick Warren]

"The Beauty Beneath: Unmasking the Realities of LIPO, 360 Tummy Tucks, and BBL Fairytales" by Latoya Johnson is intended for informational purposes only. The author is not a medical expert but shares her personal experiences and the research she has gathered on these procedures. While we acknowledge that opinions on plastic surgery can vary, this book aims to provide insight for those considering such surgeries, those who know someone contemplating them, and those who oppose them for a broader understanding. It is important to consult with qualified healthcare professionals for advice tailored to your individual circumstances and health needs.

Contents

Careformation

"CAREFORMATION IS FACTS
PROVIDED OR LEARNED WHICH IS
NECESSARY FOR THE HEALTH,
WELFARE, MAINTENANCE, AND
PROTECTION OF SOMEONE OR
SOMETHING." — [definition]

Hello, my name is Latoya and I've been a Massage Therapist for over 11 years. I enrolled in Soma Institute of Chicago for Clinical Massage Therapy where I received my certification as a therapist; from there, I took the Illinois state board test and received my License in Massage Therapy. I am a Professional Massage Therapist for relaxation and healing for the mind, body and soul. I first took an interest in post op care massages in 2018. I wanted to be part of this market to help someone's healing journey, and I can honestly say I love it. After a few years of working on post op clients, I became a client myself, which ignited my passion to learn more about post op care for plastic surgery and what it takes to have a successful, safe and healthy outcome. Before I had my surgery, many people had so much to say about how I was going to look (*amazing*), but not one person said anything about how I was going to feel and what I needed to do afterward. So, as I went through my stages of post op care with minimum knowledge of what was happening to my body and what to expect, I had to take action like never before and research every surgery experience and start listening to different board-certified doctors and their opinions on the dos and don'ts on post-op care. They are the ones who went to school for plastic surgery and can provide the most accurate information. While each doctor may have different opinions on what to do and what not to do during this period, the majority are pretty much accurate and on the same page to the road of having a successful recovery. Dealing with lymphatic post op care, you would hear different opinions all the time, and there is a lot of controversy. You essentially need to use your best judgment when it comes to this field. You are entering a world of surgical *CareFormation* that is needed for plastic/cosmetic surgery worldwide, which is meant to educate and support everyone considering or undergoing Lipo 360 BBL and Tummy tuck surgeries. In the first three months, the body is like clay. Our body goes through different stages from 3 to 12 months. So, it's very important to know how to wear your garment properly. Our body has different stages that it goes through from 3 months - 12 months. So, during these stages, it's mandatory to pay attention to how your body is developing. You must do your research on the surgeons that you are looking into. Please stop focusing on how others look because what works for someone else may not work for you.

We are all built differently (structure/body frame), so, therefore all surgeries will not come out the same way as you may want it to. After your surgery, for post-op care, the most important steps to remember for a successful, healthy recovery and great results are fajas, massages, food intake, fluids and maintaining a proper workout.

My Truth

"HONESTY IS THE FIRST CHAPTER
IN THE BOOK OF WISDOM"
— [THOMAS JEFFERSON]

I chose to get plastic surgery for myself not for anyone else including social media, reality TV, and Stars, etc. I've always been a person who cares about health and wellness. I've taught aerobics for over 11 years so working out was never an issue for me. Sometimes, the way the body is set up and the type of skin we may have makes it hard to get rid of stubborn fat. I've had two major medical surgeries, a Tubal Ligation, as well as a Hysterectomy, so my muscles were weak and no matter what I did, I was not getting the result I truly wanted for myself. I followed a strict diet for years and worked out day and night working with trainers and bodybuilders. After spending a few years researching and contemplating, whether this was something I truly wanted to do, I consulted with several plastic surgeons to seek their professional opinions on my decision and to find the best option for what I was looking for. After completing my research on doctors, searching their background and credentials and looking up their work on social media, my mind was made up. My journey started in February of 2020. I underwent my first plastic surgery procedure, the Lipo 360/Brazilian butt lift (BBL). In doing so I joined several surgery groups, which can be raw and unfiltered. Yes, I went all in, trying to make sure this was something that I was prepared for. However, it doesn't stop there. You must have a safe and clean place to go afterwards and someone to look after you for the first 5-10 days. After further research, I chose to stay in what the surgery world would call a recovery home. They usually have 24-hour around-the-clock assistance with trained professional nurses. It's in a safe and clean environment with services such as transportation, meals, medication, garment changing, bathroom assistance and much more. My second experience was 2 years later; I chose to undergo a tummy tuck because I had a hernia and it stuck out like a sore thumb, which I said to myself, *no this is not cute*. At first, I told myself repeatedly that I was not going back for plastic surgery, so, I tried going to my primary care doctor and had an ultrasound, which showed that even though the hernia was small, I would still need surgery to remove the hernia, and it would leave me with loose skin around my navel. So, there I was needing to go back since all the fat tissue had been removed, and my stomach was flat. The hernia no longer had a place to hide anymore. I didn't want to have the hernia removed to turn around and get a Tummy Tuck to tighten up my muscles. So, this time was a little different in my search for a doctor. I was now looking for doctors that specialized in Tummy Tucks and could remove my Hernia at the same time; and how well the TT scar line was done, ladies trust me, this is very important when getting a Tummy Tuck. In April of 2022, I did my second round of plastic surgery, a Tummy Tuck with my Hernia being removed and Lipo 360 removed for my sides and back. This being the second time, I didn't stay in a recovery home. I stayed in a nearby hotel and was accompanied by my mother, who was already familiar with how things should go from my first round. For both of my surgeries, I had two different surgeons, and both are board certified and licensed for over 30 plus years. My first surgeon focuses on natural looking BBLs, and my second surgeon focuses on natural looking Tummy Tucks. Both of my surgeries were done in Miami, Florida, one of the most popular states for plastic surgeons and plastic surgeries.

I understand a lot of people are non-believers and don't agree with them. There are a lot of misconceptions about having plastic surgery because of social media and the stories we hear in the news, the death tolls or people doing it for the wrong reasons. This is a decision that is critical and as humans, we can still make bad decisions. It is a part of being a lifelong learner. In this plastic surgery world, there has been a lot of bad decisions stemming from lack of research. Although people may have died from surgeries, surgeries have saved many lives as well. In most cases, people just want to look and feel good about themselves and in some instances, plastic surgery may be the only way to do that. People may have different reasons why they choose the route of Plastic Surgery, but they need to make sure it's the right decision for themselves, whether due to self-esteem issues, weight loss issues or just wanting to look a certain way etc. what we all must understand no matter what It's a common thing that in America today, which is not going anywhere. Women and men are having it done because it's affordable and technology has improved and enhanced over the years. All medical procedures are risky, but we take daily risks walking out of the door every day. Our job is to be as careful as possible, while stepping out on Faith and pursuing what our heart desires. The very people who have taken risks in their lives have a great story to tell that is inclusive of challenges. Yes plastic/cosmetic surgery is a decision that a person chooses to make. Not only does it have an impact on our outer look, but it plays a part in your mental as well. The successful and unsuccessful percentage rate of plastic surgeries are unpredictable. There are so many cases of unsuccessful surgeries as well as successful surgeries; the stories we hear about and the stories we don't hear about. Is there a right or a wrong reason for a person to choose plastic surgery? I would say yes, because your reason may clog your judgment on doing the proper research. There are so many women who choose plastic surgery for the wrong reason and will repeatedly go back because of confusion and being misled by social media or simply not being happy with who they are inside. This can cause you to make bad choices and overlook the health and safety factors of getting plastic surgery. So, if I can help at least one person have a successful and healthy journey, then I've done my job.

Raw and Uncut

> "I RESPECT PEOPLE WHO GIVE ME
> THAT RAW AND UNCUT TRUTH
> INSTEAD OF SUGAR COATING AND
> FABRICATE A LIE."
> — [lovethispic.com]

My healing process was horrible and some days I didn't even have words to describe how I was feeling. You hear and see the results afterwards, but no one ever told me about all the hell I may go through. Yes, I said what I said. I was miserable in every which way and in so much pain, I didn't understand what was going on with my body. Every day I felt like a Mack truck hit me and ran me over repeatedly. My butt felt like it was on fire at times, as if I was being dragged by a car. There was nothing I could do but endure it and after two weeks of having both surgeries, I experienced severe itching daily and throughout the entire day. The itching comes out of nowhere due to the healing of the body. This is an internal itch that is uncontrollable and can last about three months or more. I tried different methods to help sooth me, but overall, nothing really worked for me. My sleeping patterns were off because I couldn't lay on my side or back and I couldn't sit down on my butt. I had to lay flat on my stomach, which was very uncomfortable. This also triggered issues that I had going on with my body prior to my surgeries. I have two bulging discs in my lower back area, and I also have Carpal Tunnel Syndrome, a numbness and tingling in the hand and arms caused by a pinched nerve in the wrist. This would lead me to have cramps in my hands from putting on my garments daily. My back was inflamed because I had to sleep on my stomach for a year, but I learned that when getting a BBL, you can purchase what is called a BBL Pillow or chair. This helped me during my healing stages. My body went through every possible healing stage you could possibly think of, yet I still had to wear a tight and firm garment with added abdominal board, foams, and a lumbar board inside it. This may not be the experience for everyone, but the key is knowing what you may go through, in order to be mentally prepared. I also had countless Lymphatic Massages which helped with soreness, and removing excess fluid out the body. This added to my healing process, which was necessary to help reduce my swelling and the pain level. I was mentally, physically and emotionally going through it when I had both surgeries. You may say you have a high tolerance of pain and yes, I've said the same thing until I found out it doesn't matter how high your pain tolerance is; this will still take you to a whole different level of pain. I'm not telling my story to discourage you by any means. I want to provide you with all the *CareFormation* that I didn't receive. You mentally need to prepare your mind, body and soul for plastic surgery.

Was it worth it...? I would say yes in my case, because through all the pain I endured and what I had to do for my healing process, the results were a success. I've had my two rounds of plastic surgery with my two great surgeons, and I am happy with both results. It has increased my self-confidence, enhanced my outer appearance and my overall well-being. I have become more of a role model to others and inspired my family and friends that have seen the light in my eyes and how it gained me more confidence within myself. It's like when someone goes to grad school, and they work hard. There are sleepless nights, but at the end of the day, it's all worth it. You work hard so you can play hard and that's what you call a good life, doing what makes you happy. My body went through a lot of mental and physical abuse during my healing process, but looking back on my journey of plastic surgery, I am satisfied with my overall results. I've always had self-confidence, and my results of plastic surgery just gave me the complete overall look that I wanted. Ultimately, I am not looking forward to having any more plastic surgery. To be completely honest, sometimes I regret having done plastic surgery, not because of my results and the healing process, but, because of the prior physical issues that I had. My surgeries has caused me extra pain to my body daily, which is my carpal tunnel syndrome, and I have two bulging disc in my lower lumbar area, which triggered when I had to sleep flat on my stomach. But after having my surgeries and the stages of my healing process was a challenge, I remain still loyal to wearing my garments because we must keep it snatched.

30-Day Journal

"I WRITE ENTIRELY TO FIND OUT
WHAT I'M THINKING, WHAT I'M
LOOKING AT, WHAT I SEE AND
WHAT IT MEANS." — [Joan Didion]

After my first surgery, I gave myself 30 days of walking into my healing and transformation. The 1st day after surgery was my post-op follow up with the doctor and consisted of my first two lymphatic massages: one in the morning at the facility and the second at the recovery home. My pain scale was at about a 7 and my body was sore, but after my massages, I felt a lot better. My 1st week I had close to 10 lymphatic massages and daily walks. My massages hurt so badly, but I knew I needed them; the good thing about it was you felt so much better afterwards. I also had the support of my roommate. We leaned on each other along with the assistance of the nurses at the recovery home. My 2nd week I was heading home. It was the worst 3 hours of flying in my life. I was so uncomfortable. I had a full flight and what I should have done was pay extra money to be a little more comfortable and sit in the front to have extra room. I couldn't sit down; my body was sore, and I was on my knees or standing in the aisle pretty much the whole flight. After getting off the plane, my body was in distress, and I was exhausted. After getting home on the 3rd or 4th day in week 2 my body was very tender and sore. I couldn't find peace of mind and it was so hard for me to sleep. My 3rd week, I purchased everything I could search for that could make this process better and for me to able to sit without putting any pressure on my BBL/BUTT. My body was still tender and swollen, however, I was still pushing through with receiving my massages that I looked forward to every other day. I started seeing the change in my body with less swelling, bruising, and tenderness. My 4th week I was at the itching stage, which for me was the worst part of having plastic surgery. I couldn't find my comfort zone, day in and day out. Some days were good, and some days were the absolute worst. My first stage of healing was not fun, nor was it easy at all. We go through different stages; some may go through all the stages of healing, and some may not because our bodies heal differently. By weeks 5 and 6, I was better mentally and physically with time.

The Brazilian Butt Lift
(Lipo 360/BBL)

THE BRAZILIAN BUTT LIFT INVOLVES TRANSFERRING FAT FROM OTHER AREAS OF YOUR BODY TO YOUR BUTTOCKS, RESULTING IN A MORE HOURGLASS-SHAPED FIGURE WITH LARGER BUTTOCKS.

— [Facts]

The surgeon will take areas of your body with excess fat, such as the abdomen, hips, thighs or back, which will be considered fat extraction. Through liposuction, they will add it to small specific areas of your buttocks to enhance its size, shape and contour, which gives you a natural-looking outcome or for the women that want a bigger butt. The number of injections and the amount of fat injected will depend on your desired results and the surgeon's expertise. The fat is then injected into the completion areas. The incisions are usually small and well-placed to minimize visible scarring. After surgery, you should be monitored in a recovery area until the anesthesia wears off. You are to be woken up with a compression garment to reduce swelling and support the contoured areas. It's important to know that each surgeon may have their own specific techniques and variations in the procedure, so it's crucial to consult with your chosen plastic surgeon for personalized information and guidance regarding your BBL.

360 LIPO ONLY: Better known as 360 liposuction plastic surgical procedure, this procedure addresses multiple areas of the body, removing excess fat from the front and sides of the abdomen, which targets love handles or flanks, namely waist, Hips, Upper and Lower back, Upper Arms or Thighs. It helps remove stubborn fat deposits, improve body proportions and create a more contoured and balanced appearance. Lipo/360 is a popular option for individuals seeking to enhance multiple areas of their body, especially those looking for that hourglass figure or shape.

Tummy Tucks (mini & full tucks)

A TUMMY TUCK IS A PLASTIC/COSMETIC SURGICAL PROCEDURE TO IMPROVE THE APPEARANCE OF THEABDOMEN.

— [Facts]

Mini Tuck - A mini tummy tuck focuses on the lower abdomen, specifically the area below the belly button. It primarily addresses excess skin and fat in this region.

The incision made during a mini tummy tuck is typically shorter than a full tummy tuck. A mini tummy tuck focuses on skin and fat removal and may not involve significant muscle repair. It is primarily suited for individuals with minor muscle laxity limited to the lower abdomen. The incision for a mini tummy tuck is typically smaller and located low on the abdomen, resulting in a smaller scar. This procedure is less extensive than a full tummy tuck; the Mini tuck benefits someone with low muscle laxity to the lower abdomen. This is also an option for the surgeon to reposition the belly button during a mini tummy tuck. If you have good muscle tone in the upper abdomen and don't require extensive work, then the mini tummy tuck could be a possible option for you. A board-certified plastic surgeon will have to determine this based on a full evaluation.

Full tuck – A full tummy tuck often includes muscle repair, which addresses both the upper and lower abdomen. It involves more extensive tissue removal, including excess skin and fat from both areas. The procedure typically involves repositioning or reshaping the belly button and tightening of the abdominal muscles. The incision made during a full tummy tuck is longer, and usually extends from hip to hip. The surgeon tightens and repositions the abdominal muscles, particularly addressing where they separate or are weak, allowing for more extensive tissue removal and muscle repair. This can help create a firmer abdominal contour. Within many cases, the belly button is repositioned during a full tummy tuck to ensure a natural result. A full tummy tuck is mainly for those who have experienced significant changes in the abdominal area due to pregnancy, weight fluctuations or various surgeries that have damaged the muscle wall. Typically, the results of scarring are longer, but its visibility can be minimized by the right surgeons and be cut along the natural skin. It's important to consult with a board-certified plastic surgeon who specializes in abdominal contouring procedures to determine the most suitable approach for your specific case.

The Most Dangerous Plastic Surgery
Operation You Can Have

"AWARENESS AND ALERTNESS HELP US SPOT DANGERS, FIND QUICK SOLUTIONS TO PROBLEMS AND, OF COURSE, ANSWER DIFFICULT QUESTIONS WITH CONFIDENCE." — [Dr. Prem Jagasi]

It is very dangerous to take fat from one part of the body (typically abdomen) and transfer it to the buttocks. We have very small veins in the buttocks that lead to our major blood vessels that bring the blood back straight to our heart and to your lungs. In some cases, if fat enters the small blood vessels, it can lead to death. This is the primary reason it is crucial to know who your plastic surgeon is. You need to know the doctor's complete background and his track record doing surgeries. Regardless of your reasons for undergoing plastic surgery, you deserve a doctor with a flawless record of successful procedures. You often can get caught up in the sight of how good the surgeon may have done on someone and lose sight of what's most important to your wellbeing. You don't want a plastic surgeon to rush your surgery just to get to the next patient. You want a plastic surgeon that cares for all their patients' health and wellbeing.

Tragedy
Strikes

"SOMETIMES, WHEN TRAGEDY STRIKES, PEOPLE GIVE UP HOPE THAT THEY CAN EXPERCT ANYTHING MORE FROM LIFE, WHEN THE REAL QUEST IS FINDING OUT WHAT LIFE EXPECTS FROM THEM." — [Richard Paul Evans]

We hear stories all the time about the tragic losses and horrible outcomes. Undergoing plastic surgery in the hands of the wrong surgeon or not being properly cared for after surgery or doing your self-care post-op has led to countless tragedies and unforgettable situations. Deaths, Disfigurements, Paralyzed, Infections, Organ Trafficking, Immune Diseases and faulty Injections that are being put in the body are just some of the things that happen. This is something that can happen to anyone, but your percentage rate would be extremely low if the proper research is done. A lot of women travel all over to different countries looking for cheaper routes to go for plastic surgery but in a lot of these countries you have lack of licenses or no license requirements. Moreover, inexperienced doctors may be prevalent in these countries for financial gain due to lack of regulation. This also leads to a risk of being in the hands of the wrong person doing your surgery. The surgery world can be very cruel and has put a lot of people in unimaginable situations.

Question and Answer

"ASKING THE RIGHT QUESTIONS IS
JUST AS IMPORTANT AS THE
ANSWERS TO THOSE QUESTION—
WHICH IS DETERMINED BY THE
INDIVIDUAL SITUATION."
— [LATOYA JOHNSON]

This chapter contains the questions I grappled with when deciding whether to proceed with surgery. You may have different questions that could supplement these. I want to emphasize that the answers provided are based on my personal experiences and perspectives. It is crucial for you to conduct your own thorough research and seek advice tailored to your unique situation. Each individual's journey and needs are different, and consulting with qualified professionals is essential to making informed decisions about surgery.

1. Why should I wear my garments (faja)? A faja provides support to the surgical areas, helping to stabilize the tissues and contour the body.

2. What's the benefit of the faja? Minimize swelling, flatten the abdomen, reduce fluid buildup and help postoperative discomfort due to pain and soreness.

3. How long should I wear my faja? Typically, 3-6 months.

4. What's a faja burn? Friction and Moisture Contact between the skin and a tightly fitted faja for an extended period without proper care.

5. How to prevent a faja burn? Ensure that you are wearing the correct size faja with breathable materials.

Wear a cotton tank tee/shirt, wash regularly and keep clean.

6. What's the difference between a stage 1 faja and a stage 2 faja? Stage 1 faja: Typically used in the immediate post-op phase after surgical procedure and designed to be worn for the first few weeks following surgery. Stage 2 faja: Also known as a secondary maintenance faja, worn after the initial healing phase of recovery progresses. This provides a high level of compression for achieved results.

7. Do I need to wear foams and ab boards after surgery? YES, foams provide additional support for uneven skin, to contour, prevent creases of the mid-section and reduce swelling. Ab Boards provide firm compression, helping to flatten and shape the abdomen.

8. Are compression socks important? YES, for improving circulation, preventing blood Clots and deep vein

thrombosis (DVT).

9. How long do I need to wear my compression socks? The initial period is typically 10 days.

10. Why do I need Lymphatic massages after only having a Tummy tuck? Lymphatic massages focus on stimulating the lymphatic system, which helps to remove excess fluid and waste products from the body, as well as reduce swelling by promoting lymphatic drainage.

11. Tummy tuck (TT) after care? Wear a compression garment (faja); take pain medication as needed and keep the Incision area clean.

12. When to take out your drains after a Tummy Tuck (TT)? This can vary depending on your specific surgical technique used, and individual healing progress, which is important depending on your instruction from your nurse or surgeon.

13. 360 Liposuction (BBL) after care? Wear a compression garment that helps with proper skin retraction, take pain meds, have lymphatic massages, avoid direct pressure on the buttocks, sleep on your stomach or sides and use pillows or cushions to support your body's comfortable position. When sitting, use a cushion or a specially designed BBL pillow to minimize pressure on the buttocks.

14. How long do I wait to sit after a BBL? This is a time frame that varies with your surgeon, but I suggest 3 full months.

15. Can I just wear a waist trainer after my 360 BBL? NO, I don't suggest wearing a waist trainer for the first 3 months; it does not give support for the buttocks, as well as your body has to have time to form and heal.

16. Do fat cells die after a BBL? The survival rate among individuals depends on several factors. On average, 60-

80% of the transferred fat cells can survive long-term.

17. Why is it not recommended for TT and BBL to be performed at the same time? Even though they both have similarities in healing and after care, it can cause certain risks and challenges. Combining these procedures can result in more extensive recovery and increase discomfort. The recovery requirements for each procedure focus on each area with appropriate post-op care and attention.

18. How many massages should I receive after post-op surgery? Typically, a series of lymphatic massages is advised in the weeks following surgery, but it is recommended to have multiple sessions over a span of several weeks.

19. What are the effects of plastic surgery afterwards? Enhance or alter Physical appearance, Improve body function, Emotional well-being, Lifestyle, and Psychological.

20. Are Lymphatic massages important post op surgery? YES, very important; they help reduce swelling, improve circulation and enhance the healing process.

21. What's the benefit of lymphatic massages? Lymphatic massages help to stimulate lymphatic drainage, manipulate the tissues, eliminate excess fluid buildup and swelling, deliver Oxygen and nutrients to the healing tissue and remove toxin and cellular debris.

22. What is Lippo burn? Liposuction burn is a complication that can occur during or after a liposuction procedure. It involves thermal injury or damage to the skin and surrounding tissues due to excessive heat generated during the Liposuction process.

23. What causes seroma infection? After a surgery like a tummy tuck (abdominoplasty) or liposuction, if the incision does not get enough air, bacteria can develop. This can be compounded by poor wound care.

24. What is Seroma? Seroma is accumulation of fluid in a cavity created by surgery, between layers of tissue fluid buildup around the scar tissue.

25. Why should you research your surgeons? Safety and Expertise: Qualifications, experience and expertise in the specific procedure you are considering. It's crucial to ensure that your surgeon is board-certified in plastic surgery and has undergone training and education. Reputation and track record, reading reviews and testimonies from other patients, checking disciplinary actions or complaints that have been filed against the surgeon, and making sure you have the right surgeon that's fit for you.

26. Why is research very important for plastic/cosmetic surgery? Overall, research plays a vital role in ensuring your safety, satisfaction and decision making when it comes to plastic/cosmetic surgery. This knowledge allows you to make the necessary preparations, plan for

your recovery period and understand the commitment and support you may need during that time.

27. What is Infrared light therapy? The ability to promote healing and rejuvenation to the body.

28. How long should you wait to have sex after surgery? Healing time varies for different surgical procedures; it can range from a few weeks to several months.

29. How long should you wait for round 2 surgery, also known as a revision? It is crucial to allow sufficient time for your body to heal and recover from the initial surgery, which can typically be 6-12 months.

30. Should I stay at a recovery home when having surgery? Ultimately, the decision to stay in a recovery home after plastic surgery depends on your individual circumstances and preferences. Consider your specific needs, available support system, comfort level and follow the guidance of your surgeon.

31. Do you Love yourself? YES! or NO!

32. Can plastic surgery become addictive? YES!

33. Should any other doctor's besides a plastic surgeon perform plastic surgery? NO! Why? You should only have a board-certified plastic surgeon.

34. Why isn't it safe to go out of the country for plastic surgery? Because, if something goes wrong, the doctors may not have the proper medication or equipment to properly seek care for you.

35. Why do a lot of women go out of the country for plastic surgery? The procedures are much cheaper than in America.

36. Can a person have too much plastic surgery? YES!

37. Is there an actual time frame for the healing process of plastic surgery? NO! The body can take up to two years or longer to completely heal.

38. Why do you need a full medical examination and health history done before having plastic surgery? It is

especially important to be healthy and have no complications before any surgery or it could cause more harm and damage to you.

40. What is the difference between pre-op and post-op for plastic surgery? Pre-op is for those who are prepared for surgery after being cleared by both their primary care physician and the surgeon. Post op occurs after the surgery involves follow up appointment with your surgeon or nurse to ensure the surgery went well and to begin your lymphatic massages, and overall after-care.

41. When should I first start wearing my garment? Immediately after surgery, you will be awakened by the medical team with your garment on.

The Illusion

"ILLUSION IS A THING THAT IS OR IS LIKELY TO BE WRONGLY PERCEIVED OR INTERPRETED BY THE SENSES. IT IS ALSO A DECEPTIVE APPEARANCE OR IMPRESSION" — [Dictionary.com]

We seek out these surgeries to enhance our body or to make us look good. I know people look to social media and see celebrities and reality stars and their outcomes of having surgery. However, what they are not telling you or showing you is behind the scenes and the process they had to go through before they stepped out into the public's eyes. This is not a walk in the park or a comfortable situation. If you expect to be comfortable when you have done a plastic surgery procedure, then this is not for you. We all wish it were that simple and that would be all if we were living in a perfect world. You need to have a workout plan, change your eating habits, receive those Lymphatic massages and wear your garments. When you see the ones that have heavy buttocks, Deep dimples, uneven hard rock booties and a hard uneven stomach. Well, just know that they did not get the right amount of Lymphatic massages or wear a proper garment to secure a successful surgery. This also may be the result of having the wrong surgeon perform the surgery. This stems from not doing your research; I can't express this enough. Women of all ages are getting plastic surgery; It is not just a trend among young women. Plastic surgery doesn't target a particular age bracket, but there is a minimum age requirement here in the USA. Personally, it is very important to wait until you are at least 25 years of age. Because with statistics, the body beforehand can still be growing. Desperation is another reason why you should not get plastic surgery. Desperation can lead to desperate measures that can also lead to making poor decisions. When you are looking to do multiple rounds of plastic surgery, please give your body time to heal. You may look at your results and say I DON'T LIKE HOW I LOOK. Again, our bodies go through different stages and because we are not completely healed, we can look different each day. Trust the process; if your doctor performed a great job on you, then you will have a successful outcome, but still doing the aftercare work process after surgery is a must as well, so trust the Process.

Chasing an Image, You May Never Get

"OUTER BEAUTY PLEASES THE EYE. INNER BEAUTY CAPTIVATES THE HEART." — [Mandy Hale]

It is ok to have a wish picture, but just know that your outcome may not appear the way you may want it to be.

Our body structure is made different from one another. So,

what works for me may not work for you and what works for you may not work for me. We come in all shapes and sizes. This is why it's very important to not just focus on how someone else looks. Some doctors are good at what they do but may have a certain type of BMI woman that they are good with working with for a better result. We also have different skin types, and our bone structures are different as well. You basically need a plastic surgeon that knows what you need and knows how to operate and perform properly. You want a plastic surgeon to tell you the truth about what they can and cannot do for you, instead of telling you what you want to hear just to take your money.

Another important point when searching for the right doctor is to consider their experience with patients of your ethnic background. You don't want a doctor who rarely works with patients of your ethnicity because our bodies can be shaped differently, and the results may not meet your expectations. We often hear about family, friends, or reality stars who had great results with a particular doctor, but going to the same surgeon might yield different outcomes for us. It's important to understand that what worked for someone else might not work the same way for us.

Plastic Surgery must be taken seriously for more than one reason, and we must stop looking at it as just an image.

Reality

"REALITY IS ONE OF THE
POSSIBILITIES I CANNOT AFFORD
TO IGNORE." — [Leonard Cohen]

What makes plastic surgery a wrong decision is when you are not doing it for yourself. When this happens, it becomes psychological, and you will never be happy with the permanent decision you made. Your mind starts playing tricks on you and every time you get plastic surgery, nothing will ever be right to you. This will lead you to constantly second guess your looks and you will keep getting more surgeries, which can lead to you having a botched procedure. This can become so overwhelming that you may lose sight of caring about your health, focusing only on your appearance and going to risky lengths to achieve your desired look, which can lead you down a dangerous path. Plastic surgery can be very expensive, but you can find board certified surgeons that have specials and are very affordable for these procedures instead of looking for a shortcut in Prices and going out the country to an unknown place, possibly risking your life. When getting plastic surgery, remember the aftercare. You can't just pay for the procedures and not have money for your aftercare/self-care; you don't want to cheat yourself out of your post-op self-care.

Your aftercare/Self-care is the most important part of having plastic surgery. So, not only will you need money for having plastic surgery, but you will need to have money set aside for your self-care. Once you give your body time to heal and form, this would give you your complete look if the surgeon did their job properly. Plastic surgery can also become highly addictive, leading to a mentally dangerous rabbit hole. A person may undergo countless surgeries one after another from top to bottom without considering the high-risk they are subjecting their bodies too. I'm not trying to scare anyone out of having plastic surgery, but if I can scare you into going in the right direction for a healthy, successful and beautiful outcome, then I have done my job. Plastic surgery can be stressful and time consuming and I know a lot of us want to rush and get the procedure done. However, we must remember this is a life changing game changer for us, so we need to make sure that we have all the resources and tools before making such a permanent decision to our beautiful bodies. Plastic surgery has become extremely popular and highly successful for surgeons. As a result, you have a lot of doctors that are not capable of properly executing plastic surgery or doing the kind of surgery you want which can be very dangerous and life threatening. I repeat, before taking this risk, you must ask yourself: Is this the right doctor for what I want, and does this doctor have the proper credentials as a board-certified surgeon? We also need to consider our own health issues and whether plastic surgery is worth the potential complications. Sometimes, the desire for the procedure leads people to uncertified doctors or those with no medical background, increasing the risk of something going wrong. The lack of funds a person may not have for the surgery you may want to take a turn down the short cut road to receive plastic surgery this is also, not a safe way to go. We know the saying you get what you pay for and in some cases that is an understatement.

Was It Worth It?

> "FOR WHAT IT'S WORTH IT'S NEVER TOO LATE TO BE WHOEVER YOU WANT TO BE. I HOPE YOU LIVE A LIFE YOU'RE PROUD OF AND IF YOU FIND THAT YOU'RE NOT, I HOPE YOU HAVE THE STRENGTH TO START OVER."
> — [F. Scott Fitzgerald]

This is a question you would need to ask yourself, because I did. Everybody's experience will be different, and everyone's impact from plastic surgery will be different. This is a sensitive subject to some, but it's needed and it's something that you must know. **PLEASE ANSWER THESE SURVEY QUESTIONS.**

1. **Initial Motivation:** Why did you decide to undergo plastic surgery (lipo 360, tummy tucks or BBL)? Were there specific aspects of your appearance or life that motivated this decision?

2. **Expectations**: What were your expectations before undergoing the procedures? Did you have a specific outcome in mind, and if so, did it align with reality?

3. **Research and Decision-Making**: How much research did you conduct before deciding on plastic surgery? Did you consult with multiple professionals and gather diverse opinions?

4. **Pre-Procedure Preparation**: How well were you prepared physically and emotionally before

surgery? Were there any challenges or surprises during the preparation phase?

5. **Procedure Experience**: Can you describe your experience during and immediately after the plastic surgery procedures? Were there any unexpected or particularly challenging moments?

6. **Recovery Process**: How would you describe the overall recovery process? Were there any aspects of recovery that were more challenging than you anticipated?

7. **Results and satisfaction**: Are you satisfied with the results of the plastic surgery? How do the actual results compare to your expectations?

8. **Psychological Impact**: Have you noticed any changes in your self-esteem or confidence since the surgery? How has the experience affected your overall well-being?

9. **Social and Professional Impact**: Have you observed any changes in how you are perceived by others, both personally and professionally? How have your relationships with friends, family or colleagues been affected?

10. **Reflection and Advice**: Looking back, do you believe the plastic surgery was worth it for you? What advice would you give to someone considering similar procedures?

Please be advised that what you have presented as your answers are your exact feelings and experience and this will not be at any cost to you as a liability.

About the Author

"AUTHORS DO NOT CHOOSE A STORY TO WRITE, THE STORY CHOOSES US." — [Richard Denney]

Latoya Johnson is a dedicated and passionate individual hailing from the vibrant city of Chicago, Illinois. She was born under the roof of the Linda Spraggins (*her mother*), and she is the proud sibling of two brothers and three sisters. In addition, Latoya is a devoted mother of two children, which has added another layer of love and purpose to her life.

Latoya's journey is marked by significant accomplishments that she holds dear to her heart. After completing her education at Jones Metro Business Prep High School, she pursued her passion for massage therapy at the Soma Institute of Massage Therapy in her hometown of Chicago. This educational pursuit allowed her to gain valuable skills and knowledge in the field.

One of her proudest achievements is her attendance at the Clinical School of Massage Therapy, where she honed her skills and developed a deep understanding of the art of massage. This expertise led her to write her first book, which focuses on the importance and safety of lymphatic massages.

Through her writing, she aims to share her knowledge and experience, contributing to the well-being of others.

In addition to her educational and professional journey, Latoya is the CEO of her own business, "Queen of Therapy." This business reflects her dedication to providing top-notch therapeutic services to her clients, and it allows her to take charge and make a positive impact in her community.

Outside of her career and achievements, Latoya finds solace and joy in the art of dance. It is her favorite hobby and a source of personal expression and relaxation. Her deep-seated passion for helping others shines through in her work and her dedication to her family and friends, who would describe her as fun, loyal, and the life of the party. Latoya's secret, however, is that she is a very emotional person, which adds depth and authenticity to her relationships and interactions with those around her.